IMAGES
of America
THE 1964–1965
NEW YORK WORLD'S FAIR

The 1964–1965 New York World's Fair was an immense undertaking. In addition to the many pavilions seen here, the project included the construction of the highways to the fairgrounds, extension of railroad lines, and the development of a new marina. Nearby Shea Stadium was built at the same time.

IMAGES of America
THE 1964–1965 NEW YORK WORLD'S FAIR

Bill Cotter and Bill Young

ARCADIA
PUBLISHING

Copyright © 2004 by Bill Cotter and Bill Young
ISBN 978-1-5316-2105-6

Published by Arcadia Publishing
Charleston, South Carolina

Library of Congress Catalog Card Number: 2004103581

For all general information contact Arcadia Publishing at:
Telephone 843-853-2070
Fax 843-853-0044
E-mail sales@arcadiapublishing.com
For customer service and orders:
Toll-Free 1-888-313-2665

Visit us on the Internet at www.arcadiapublishing.com

Contents

Introduction ... 7

1. The Master Builder ... 9
2. The Near Tomorrow ... 13
3. Shrinking Globe, Expanding Universe ... 23
4. Exploring the Space Age ... 29
5. The Fair's Showman ... 37
6. Populuxe and Pop Art ... 51
7. Cold Warfair ... 67
8. A World's Fair? ... 73
9. Something for Everybody ... 85
10. The Beat Goes On ... 107

Wonders awaited those holding a ticket to the fair. Prices were reasonable: $2 for adults, $1 for children—and that was before any group discounts. Although slightly more expensive in 1965, when compared to the price of today's theme parks, the fair truly was a bargain.

INTRODUCTION

I cannot remember the actual date of my first visit to the fair. I really wish I could, because that visit and the ones to follow had a profound effect on me. I was 12 years old in 1964, and my first impression of the sights and sounds of Flushing Meadows made me realize that the adults of the time must really have lost their minds. Why else, I wondered, would they build such a magical world and plan to tear it down in two years?

During the run of the fair, I kept waiting for the grownups to come to their senses, but just in case they did not, I went as often as I could. There were visits with my family, with the Boy Scouts, and with friends and their families. Then, much to my surprise and joy, my parents agreed that I could go there on my own as long as I took one of my younger brothers. More trips followed, and my coin collection vanished in the pursuit of tickets and Bel-Gem waffles.

I have always been a collector of souvenirs from places I visit, and the fair was certainly a great spot to add new treasures to my collection. Today, 40 years and several moves later, I still have the box of souvenirs I gathered at the fair. Opening it and flipping through the brochures, maps, and photographs is like a time machine for me—a return to a world where the future was promised to be bright and wonderful.

I have also been interested in photography as long as I can remember. I have spent countless hours reliving the days of the fair and recalling half-forgotten moments and sights as I spot them again on film, and I hope the photographs in this book work the same magic for you.

As we know, the world leaders of 1964 and 1965 did not share my visions and plans for the fair, and by 1966, it was all gone. Although I can no longer walk past the pavilions, watch the waving flags, or enjoy the fireworks over the Fountain of the Planets, I still have to smile when I think of the fair. After all, my visits there played a large part in my later working for Disney, where I met my wife. She never visited the fair herself, but happily, she indulges me in my efforts to travel back in time.

—Bill Cotter
www.billcotter.com
April 2004

I loved *The Jetsons*, that space-age cartoon series featuring the 21st-century Jetson family, their dog, Astro, and faithful maid, Rosie the robot. From the night the television show first aired in 1962, I could not wait to grow up so I could eat a breakfast of blue pills, put on my silver jump suit, hop into my flying car, and travel to my high-rise office-on-a-pole to spend my day working on my own computer. What a future *that* was going to be!

A few years ago, a commercial for a computer brand aired on network television. In the advertisement, a family of four is shown driving through a city in a sleek minivan. Mom and dad are in the front seat, while son and sis are in the back seat, chatting away with friends on their cell phones. Dad pulls up to a school, and the kids head off to class with a cheerful wave. Next stop: a shopping center. As dad drops mom off for her day with friends, he hands her his debit card. With a sly smile, mom snatches his wallet instead and heads off. Dad just chuckles and continues on to work. He arrives there and travels up the side of his high-rise office building in a glass elevator. Once inside his office, he leans back in his chair and props his feet up on his desk as his laptop computer boots up for a day of work.

If the volume were turned down on the television, the advertisement would have appeared to be a rather nondescript commentary on the life of today's ordinary family. It had no words. The message was conveyed through the background music. What was playing? Why, the theme song from *The Jetsons*, of course. That is when I stopped being disappointed that my life was not filled with flying cars and silver jump suits and realized that I *am* George Jetson after all.

I have never stopped being fascinated with predictions of life in the future, and there has never been a greater display of ideas for a Jetson-esque life than was presented at that space-age extravaganza called the 1964–1965 New York World's Fair. In 2000, I launched a Web site called www.nywf64.com to indulge and to share my interest in that amazing fair. The Web site has proven its popularity. It seems I am not the only one fascinated with past predictions of life in the future. From the Web site has come my friendship with Bill Cotter and this affiliation with Arcadia Publishing and the book you hold in your hands.

Today, I spend my workday in front of a computer screen. A bright blue Pontiac Firebird is as close as I have come to a flying car. Breakfast is not in the form of blue pills, but my nutrition is better than ever. My jeans and sweatshirts are a lot more comfortable than a silver jump suit. In some ways, my life in the future is even better than George Jetson's. I still want a Rosie the robot, though.

—Bill Young
www.nywf64.com
April 2004

One

The Master Builder

The old S.O.B. does it again.

—The *Saturday Evening Post*,
May 23, 1964, 237th Year, No. 20

World's fairs are, by their very nature, special events. Vast resources must be brought to bear in the design, building, and operation of something that is quite transitory in nature. There is great excitement when the fairs are announced and even greater excitement when they open. However, after they close, there is usually little left to mark their existence other than a few leftover buildings and millions of happy memories. Along the way, the fairs entertain, educate, and amuse. They also provide an opportunity for architects to go wild, countries to show off, and companies to advertise as never before.

The 1964–1965 New York World's Fair was one of the biggest international extravaganzas and set records for its size and cost. More than 51 million visitors enjoyed the sights, sounds, and tastes of the fair during two summer seasons. However, before any of the guests could walk through the gate, a tremendous amount of work was required to bring the fair to fruition.

In the late 1950s, a group of businessmen and politicians banded together to search for a way to celebrate the 300th anniversary of the founding of New York City, in 1664. After numerous plans were floated and discarded, the choice was made to host a new world's fair at the same location as the earlier 1939–1940 New York World's Fair: Flushing Meadows. What a fair this new one was to be!

While the 1939–1940 fair was a massive undertaking on its own, the new fair was to be bigger, better, and more breathtaking. It was going to show the world that New York City was the center of American business, and that America was the center of the world's economy. Heady with enthusiasm, the initial planners soon realized that they needed someone very special indeed to bring their ambitious dreams to reality.

The man they chose was Robert Moses, a bureaucrat with an amazing track record for massive building projects. People who grew up outside New York City may have a hard time grasping just how powerful a man Moses was. Although never elected to public office, he was responsible for more public works projects than any of the elected officials under whom he served. He held a wide range of positions for an amazing number of government agencies and built a vast network of highways, bridges, tunnels, and dams over the years. He was also the longtime head of the city's parks department, which put him in the perfect position to use the new fair to complete his long-dreamed-of park in Flushing Meadows.

The 1939–1940 New York World's Fair, famous for its stylized architecture and Trylon and Perisphere theme symbols, had been built on a former ash dump in a then desolate section of Queens. One of the goals of that fair had been the creation of a new city park to benefit the local residents. Yet, when the fair ran out of money, the park was only partly completed.

Robert Moses poses for his official fair photograph, with his hand resting on a large model of the Unisphere, the theme symbol for the new fair that he was chosen to build. It is fitting in many ways that he was selected for the job, as he had been one of the driving forces behind the earlier fair. Frustrated when that fair closed without completing the promised park, he had long wanted to see his pet project finished on the site of the fair. Now, 25 years later, he had another chance.

Fueled by investors who were sure that Robert Moses could repeat the successes he had enjoyed at the helm of so many government agencies, the 1964–1965 New York World's Fair Corporation went into high gear. Construction is seen here under way on the massive General Motors Pavilion. Even though the structure was temporary, it featured a steel framework worthy of a building intended to last for years.

One of the first things Robert Moses announced was that the new fair would follow much of the physical layout of the first one, thereby allowing the builders to use the infrastructure already in place. The Unisphere, theme symbol for the new fair, was to be placed on the site of the first fair's Trylon and Perisphere. Streets and walkways were to remain in their current locations as much as possible, and any changes made were to be for the ultimate benefit of the park. Here, the Ford Pavilion takes shape.

Although critics attacked many of the decisions made by Robert Moses, in the end much of what he did was proven to be right. In some areas, such as his controversial awarding of contracts and handling of labor issues, Moses did err, but such is the advantage of hindsight. Given the politics involved, it is doubtful that anyone else would have enjoyed the same success that Moses did in building his fair. None of the controversies mattered much to fair visitors once they arrived at the site. Seen here is Gotham Plaza, the main entrance to the fair.

Sadly, when the last guest had departed and the fanciful buildings were gone again from Flushing Meadows, Robert Moses' grand park again remained incomplete. Like its predecessor, this fair also ran out of money to complete the park. Despite that failure, Moses left a legacy that will live on in the memories of those who attended his triumph at the former ash dump. Will there ever be another fair like that one? It is doubtful, but if there is to be one, Robert Moses will be a tough act to follow.

Two

THE NEAR TOMORROW

The answers we seek will be found in the near tomorrow. . . . Let us explore together the future. A future not of dreams but of reality. For much of what we are about to see is even now beyond the promise and well on its way to tomorrow's world.

—The General Motors Futurama ride narration

On October 4, 1957, the Soviet Union launched the world's first artificial satellite into orbit around the earth. Weighing less than 200 pounds, the basketball-sized satellite was named *Sputnik I*. In the brief span of one lifetime, mankind had advanced from the era of the Wright brothers' flyer to the very threshold of space. He had also invented the atomic bomb. If such progress could be made in such a short span of time, what other wonders lay ahead in the near tomorrow? In 1964, the United States was in the midst of an era called the space age. Much more than just a catchword for the early era of space exploration, the phrase describes a time when the country needed to believe that the amazing advances in science and technology would soon lead to a future of limitless promise. The alternative could be the very extinction of humanity.

The 1964–1965 New York World's Fair was all about the promise that science, technology, and a free society were the keys to building a better tomorrow. The fair offered many predictions for a wonderful future that seemed to be just around the corner. The most elaborate display was General Motors' Futurama, the most popular attraction at the fair.

On the Futurama ride, visitors seated three abreast in moving chairs rode past six detailed dioramas that depicted life in the future. Ranging in size from miniature sets to life-sized tableaux, the scenes pictured the conquering of outer space and the ocean depths; the taming of jungles, deserts, and ice shelves; and the advent of technology that would brighten the homes and cities of tomorrow. An inspiring narration played through speakers in the headrests throughout the 14-minute journey into the future.

With a two-year attendance of 29 million, more than 60 percent of visitors to the fair saw the show. Futurama was an updated version of General Motors' equally popular Futurama ride at the 1939–1940 New York World's Fair. Although Futurama I depicted life in then far-off 1960, the new Futurama simply said its predictions were already "beyond the promise" and well on their way to becoming a reality.

What became of the future that Futurama promised? Predictions of moon bases and vacation hotels beneath the seas proved to be the stuff of *Popular Science* stories and Jetson-esque cartoons, but to Futurama's great credit, its fanciful predictions (along with the possibilities presented by other space-age oriented displays at the fair) led thousands of young visitors to dream that they could be a part of making an exciting future. Now, those youngsters have become scientists, engineers, and creative geniuses working to find the answers for today's near tomorrow.

The General Motors Pavilion was one of the largest buildings at the fair. Approximately 4,000 tons of structural steel and 10,500 cubic yards of concrete went into its construction. The distinctive canopy that served as the pavilion's entrance soared 10 stories over a reflecting pool and was visible for miles. The central section of the building housed the popular Futurama ride, and the circular structure held General Motors product displays.

It has been said that the towering canopied entrance to the General Motors Pavilion was designed to mimic the tail fin features found on automobiles of the late 1950s and early 1960s. Whether this is true or not is open to speculation. The canopy was, however, an eye-catching feature of the massive pavilion. At night, colored pastel lights projected upward against the surface of the facade, creating a remarkable and beautiful sight.

Futurama was the star of the show. General Motors stylists created scenes in which the innovations they predicted were shown advancing the fortune of all mankind. Comfortably seated in moving chairs, Futurama time travelers passed an orbiting space station on their way to the moon. A lunar base was the first stop on their journey into the future.

On the surface of the moon, lunar rovers with large balloonlike wheels roll by. Mankind's first triumph in the conquering of outer space is to establish bases from which further space explorations can be launched.

Lunar bases, outposts of communication and supply for earthling explorers, are constructed to withstand the temperature extremes of the moon's surface. The Futurama train then turns away from the moon and back toward the earth, to its southern polar icecap and Antarctica, once considered as remote as the moon.

Antarctica is filled with scientific communities dedicated to research. It is home to Weather Central, where technicians gather data on climate changes born in the Antarctic winds. From beneath Antarctica's ice, the Futurama traveler journeys to warmer waters to see how mankind harvests an abundance of food from the seas.

Three-quarters of the earth is covered by oceans, and in those deeps, mankind discovers vast food supplies of plant and aquatic life. In fact, there is food enough to feed more than seven times the population of the earth, and the Futurama traveler sees examples of underwater farming.

Even in the future, man does not live on plankton alone. New vacation destinations are developed beneath the seas. Here is Hotel Atlantis, set in an underwater paradise. Aquacopters float by as the Futurama travelers learn that they will soon be able to spend a weekend of relaxation in such an idyllic setting.

17

The mountains, like the jungle, were once barriers to development. Now, mankind has not only spanned them with superhighways but also developed them with spectacular mountain dwellings, inviting the humans of the near tomorrow to live in a world of awesome beauty.

How to feed the population of an ever-growing world—the Futurama traveler sees a whole desert green with growing plants. Ocean water is desalinated and used to irrigate the world's deserts.

Perched high atop a mountainside, the Home of Tomorrow is an open concept design, seemingly a part of the environment it occupies. Looking closely, Futurama travelers can see that the lucky resident has a sleek new red General Motors Firebird IV parked in the carport below the home.

The Futurama voyager now arrives via the Continental Highway at the entrance to the City of Tomorrow. Vehicle travel on the highway is computer controlled, and cars are electronically spaced for safety.

19

The City of Tomorrow is a great center of commerce. Towering modern skyscrapers, covered moving walkways, and safe and swift and efficient transportation are all a part of the wonders that await the Futurama traveler in tomorrow's modern metropolis.

Despite all its technological wonders, the City of Tomorrow still has room for tradition and faith. A beautiful cathedral is nestled in a plaza among the towering skyscrapers in the heart of the city.

The time traveler flies high above a glittering City of Tomorrow, and the Futurama journey comes to an end. "The present is but an instant between an infinite past and a hurrying future. . . . Technology can point the way to a future of limitless promise, but man must chart his own course into tomorrow. A course that frees the mind and the spirit as it improves the well-being of mankind."

In the Avenue of Progress, General Motors presented new ideas and products for the near tomorrow. The Firebird IV, newest in a series of experimental gas turbine-driven cars, anticipated the day when a driver could turn over the car's controls to an automatic, programmed guidance system and travel in comfort and safety on a superhighway.

Although most of the futuristic concept cars were never available for sale, visitors browsed through a large selection of current General Motors models, as seen in this section of the Pontiac display.

The central courtyard exhibit in General Motors' circular Product Plaza was that of the Frigidaire Division, whose displays included household appliances such as refrigerators and stoves. The Product Plaza spotlighted General Motors' diversity in manufacturing by exhibiting products from its many commercial divisions.

Three

SHRINKING GLOBE, EXPANDING UNIVERSE

Man's Achievements on a Shrinking Globe in an Expanding Universe.

—1964–1965 New York World's Fair Dedication Statement

It is the largest representation of Earth ever made. Standing some 12 stories high and constructed of bridge-strength stainless steel, Unisphere depicts Earth as it would appear from 6,000 miles out in space. It was the fair's official theme center, symbolizing Peace through Understanding and representing mankind's interdependence on a planet that the space age was making ever smaller. The three rings encircling the globe represent the orbits of the first artificial satellites launched into space. Truly the centerpiece of the fair, Unisphere was constructed and presented as a gift by the United States Steel Corporation.

Unisphere was not the only structure suggested as a symbol for the fair. Portland Cement offered to build a huge concrete star-viewing platform called Galaxon for the theme center, but the bright lights of the city and the fair would have made such a structure impractical. Another suggestion was a spiraling tower, dubbed Journey to the Stars, which was topped by floating star-shaped balloons. The World's Fair Corporation chose Unisphere over other designs because it was felt its concept would be more readily understood by the average fairgoer.

As originally conceived, Unisphere was to have rotated on a base hidden by jets of water spray, but the sheer size and weight of the globe made this impractical. In the end, the water sprays became the lovely Fountains of the Continents, and an orbiting Earth was suggested by innovative lighting and fountain effects rather than by mechanical means. During the fair, lights embedded in the steel continents marked the capitals of the nations of the world.

After the fair closed, Unisphere remained on the fair site as a permanent feature of the improved Flushing Meadows–Corona Park. As fair president Robert Moses remarked at the start of construction for Unisphere, "[It will] remind succeeding generations of a pageant of surpassing interest and significance." Granted landmark status in 1989, it stands today a gleaming symbol of New York City, of the borough of Queens, and of the era that was the space age.

Mounted on a 70-ton tripod base, Unisphere is like a beachball balanced on a golf tee. It could not have been created before the advent of computers because the calculations that went into its design could not have been accomplished without them. Since Unisphere is open, the continents act like sails and create enormous stresses on the structure. The structure had to be designed to withstand winds of up to 100 miles per hour in case of hurricanes.

In order for the globe to look realistic, no diagonal bracing was used between the open areas of latitude and longitude. Without such bracing, Unisphere would require supports that were heavier and bulkier, detracting from its light and attractive appearance. The lower meridians are actually welded girders that support the entire structure. Unisphere is an amazing feat of engineering.

Some 50 steel guy wires connect each of the three-ton orbit rings to Unisphere, much like spokes tie a bicycle wheel rim to its axle. The wires are so strong and light that the orbital rings seem to float above the surface of the globe.

Flags of many nations wave from the poles along the Court of Nations as visitors stroll beneath Unisphere. As the fair's theme center, Unisphere was designed to be a permanent reminder of mankind's aspirations for peace through understanding, as well as a symbol of achievement in an expanding universe. Along with the Eiffel Tower, Space Needle, and Brussels' Atomium, it is among but a handful of surviving symbols of past expositions.

Unisphere was ringed by the Fountains of the Continents. This remarkable fountain effect consisted of 96 water jets projecting vertical streams of water from 8 to 40 feet in height, simulating an advancing wave action. Unisphere seemingly floated in space, and the rising and falling motion of the advancing wave pattern suggested a rotation of the globe. A modified version of the fountains was created for post-fair use.

This closeup of Central America shows how multiple layers of stainless steel were used to represent mountains. The textured skin of the Unisphere helped keep it from being a blinding mirror.

Although the fountains surrounding the Unisphere are usually silent, recent renovations have allowed them to be used for special events such as the U.S. Open tennis tournament held at the nearby Arthur Ashe Stadium.

Dusk falls, and the lights come on at the fair. Unisphere's lighting effects were designed to resemble the day-night cycle of the earth. The effect was accomplished by special lighting equipment mounted on five light towers that surrounded the globe at a 200-foot radius. Light movement simulated a setting sun. The entire performance was automated with synchronized timers to control the lighting.

In addition to the special lighting that suggested rotation, the capitals of the nations were represented by bright bulbs in the steel continents. Each light canister contained four bulbs. When one burned out, a new bulb automatically moved into position to take its place, eliminating the need for mechanics to keep the lights burning during the fair. After the fair closed, all of the special lighting was removed or simply disconnected.

Four

EXPLORING THE SPACE AGE

I believe that this nation should commit itself to achieving the goal, before this decade is out, of landing a man on the Moon and returning him safely to the Earth.

—Pres. John F. Kennedy, May 25, 1961

The 1964–1965 New York World's Fair opened at the midpoint of the Russo-American race to see which country could be the first to land a man on the moon. It was a matter of cold war survival, in which one country dared not allow the other to have a mastery of space. Project Mercury missions had ended in 1963, and with Project Gemini ushering in space walks and space docking, America appeared close to fulfilling Pres. John F. Kennedy's challenge to put a man on the moon before decade's end. Men named Alan Shepard, John Glenn, and Scott Carpenter became American heroes, their missions televised and watched by millions and their safe return to earth celebrated with ticker-tape parades. Youngsters drank Tang, just like the astronauts. Words, phrases, and acronyms like Telstar, Saturn V boosters, and LEM became a part of everyday conversation.

With all of this interest in things celestial, many exhibits brought fairgoers face to face with the space age. Visitors saw demonstrations of space-docking techniques at the Hall of Science. No less than 31 space vehicles were on loan and displayed by NASA and the Defense Department in the U.S. Space Park. A Buck Rogers–type character actually flew over the fairgrounds with a rocket pack strapped to his back. General Motors' Futurama predicted that the United States would be establishing lunar bases. The Bell Telephone System, the Hall of Science, and the state of New Jersey displayed mock-ups of the communications satellite Telstar. Missouri exhibited its contributions to the space program with a display of a spacewalking astronaut floating above the Gemini capsule. At the West Virginia pavilion, visitors saw demonstrations of the radio astronomy dishes at the Green Bank Observatory, where astronomers searched for signs of other intelligent life in the universe.

Space themes were everywhere. Kodak had a roof called the Moon Deck. Fairgoers strolled by sculptures of Donald DeLeu's *The Rocket Thrower* and Theodore Rozek's *Forms in Space*. The Transportation and Travel Pavilion featured a Moon Dome theater where the Cinerama film *To the Moon and Beyond* played to capacity audiences. From turbine car to Amphicar to monorail to rocket ship, the fair showed that mankind was on the move toward an exciting tomorrow.

The Hall of Science was constructed as a permanent part of Flushing Meadows–Corona Park. A demonstration of docking spacecraft played out high above floor level in the Great Hall, where thousands of pieces of cobalt blue stained glass were set into the undulating concrete walls, giving visitors the illusion of being in deep space. Lower-level exhibits included Atomsville USA, where children discovered the benefits of atomic energy.

Occupying a full two acres outside the Hall of Science, the U.S. Space Park gave fairgoers the opportunity to study America's space program up close. Full-scale replica rockets like this Mercury-Atlas booster and Thor-Delta launch vehicle were displayed alongside actual spacecraft that had been used in the space program. Fiberglass panels enclosed the park and displayed written descriptions of the exhibits.

The largest piece of NASA equipment on display was a mock-up of a Saturn V Boattail, the first-stage propulsion section of the rockets used to launch Apollo spacecraft toward the moon. The Boattail stood 51 feet tall and gave fairgoers a good idea of the massive size of the rockets needed to launch lunar missions. This realistic-looking piece of space equipment was actually constructed of metal sheeting over plywood.

The lunar excursion module, or LEM, was on display in the U.S. Space Park. This vehicle was used to transport two astronauts from the orbiting Apollo command module to the surface of the moon. Once the mission was completed, the bottom section of the LEM served as a launch pad, with only the top portion returning from the lunar surface to the command module.

Here is a view of the Apollo command module on display in the U.S. Space Park. This three-man vehicle was used in the latter part of the decade to transport American astronauts to lunar orbit. In the background stands the LEM, or lunar excursion module, that carried astronauts to the surface of the moon.

West Virginia displayed its contributions to science and technology that were creating a better tomorrow for all Americans. Although the stuff of science fiction novels, the exhibit explained the importance of the Green Bank Observatory, where gigantic radio telescope dishes were scanning the sky, listening for signals that indicated the existence of other intelligent life in the universe.

This is the enormous 96-foot-high Moon Dome of the Transportation and Travel Pavilion. It had a plastic covering that formed an accurate relief map of the surface of the moon. The dome was actually a Cinerama theater, in which the Dutch airline KLM presented a movie titled *To the Moon and Beyond*, a space show that turned fairgoers into interplanetary commuters.

Other exhibitors inside the Transportation and Travel Pavilion included Trans World Airlines. Its display was a large model of a supersonic transport plane, or SST, in full Starstream livery. The SST was touted as the next advance in air travel. Although the British and French eventually built the Concorde for supersonic air travel, plans for an American SST were eventually scrapped.

33

Space themes seemed to be everywhere, as fairgoers strolled along the Court of the Astronauts past *The Rocket Thrower,* by Donald DeLeu. One of the fair's principal works of art, *The Rocket Thrower* was surpassed in importance only by Unisphere and the display of the sculpture *Pieta.* It even appeared on a U.S. postage stamp commemorating the 1964–1965 New York World's Fair. *The Rocket Thrower* remains in place today as a reminder of the fair.

Rocket ships were not the only mode of space-age travel on display at the fair. Many urban planners were convinced that monorails were sure to be the most practical and innovative form of land-based mass transit in the near future. At the fair, American Machine and Foundry (AMF) Corporation constructed a working example of such a system. The suspended monorails traveled in a continuous loop around the fair's Amusement Area.

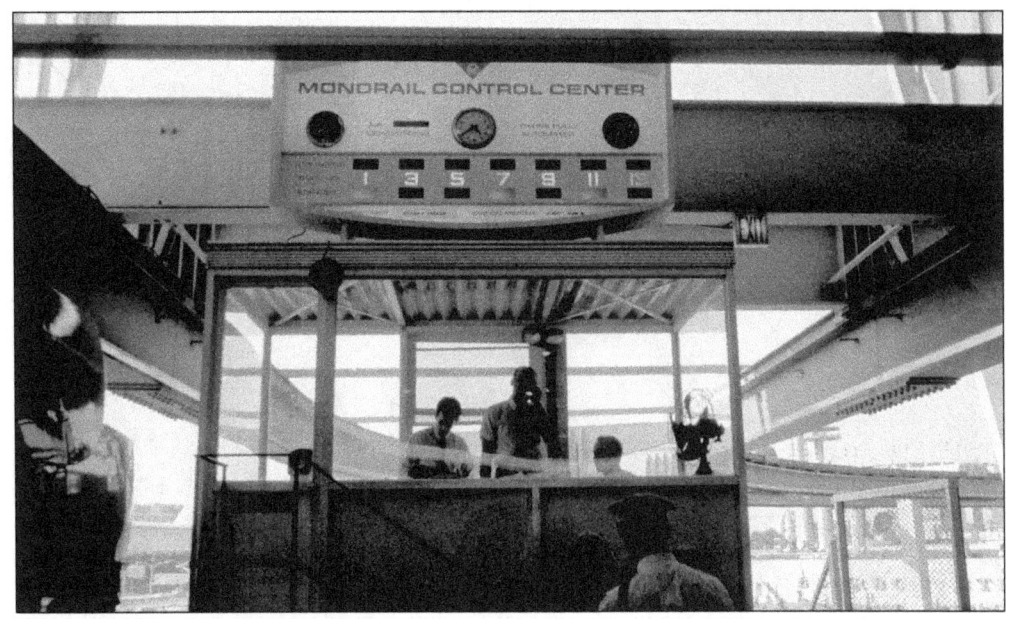

This is a view of the control center in the AMF monorail station. Although automatic controls governed train arrival and departure and opened coach doors for passengers, crew members were added to reassure nervous passengers. AMF had seven two-car trains operating on tracks suspended 40 feet above the fairgrounds. Each train had a capacity of 80 passengers and moved at a mere six miles per hour, hardly a realistic display of the potential of monorail transportation.

This view was taken approaching the AMF monorail station. Although they could utilize existing space along highways and were safe and fast and nearly noiseless, monorails were an idea that did not catch on after the space age ended. AMF had high hopes of building systems like this one across the country. Other than the few examples that exist today at airports and amusement parks, monorails remain a space-age dream.

Magazine articles had long been promising that the future would herald the advent of flying cars, thus eliminating congestion on modern highways. Perhaps the most unusual of the fair's many displays of futuristic transportation was the Amphicar. It had a waterproof bottom and sides—and twin propellers. Fairgoers taking this car for a spin wound up in Meadow Lake. Amphicars seem to have suffered the same fate as monorails.

No more affordable to fairgoers than the Amphicar, James Bond's famous Aston Martin DB5 was fresh from the hit film *Goldfinger*. Visitors were treated to demonstrations of its unique accessories, which included machine guns, oil slicks, a bulletproof shield, and an ejector seat.

Five

THE FAIR'S SHOWMAN

*We have one piece of real estate left at the World's Fair.
I've got a little idea for a boat ride.*

—Walt Disney

Of all of the designers, architects, and businesspeople who built the fair, Walt Disney was perhaps second only to Robert Moses in making it such a memorable experience. He and his staff created four of the most popular shows at the fair and thus revolutionized the theme park business. Along the way he also proved that there was a market for Disneyland-style entertainment on the East Coast, which helped solidify his thoughts for what later became Walt Disney World.

The success of Disneyland made Disney a natural choice for companies looking for a soft-sell method to showcase their products at the fair. Disney initially met with General Motors to talk about creating a show for the company. However, General Motors decided instead to do the Futurama ride and suggested that he talk to Ford, which had yet to announce its plans. Disney rose to the occasion by designing the Magic Skyway, in which guests in new Ford convertibles traveled back to the days of the dinosaurs. The propulsion system used for that show, and the dinosaurs themselves, are still in use today.

The fair marked the introduction of Disney's Audio-Animatronic figures, the most lifelike of which was a re-creation of Abraham Lincoln for the state of Illinois. The pavilion staff was faced by audience members who, convinced that a live actor was playing the part, sometimes tried to prove their point by throwing things at the robotic president. Disney's most popular show at the fair, General Electric's Carousel of Progress, started out as a potential expansion of Disneyland to be called Edison Square. That project was reworked into a unique presentation in which audiences traveled in a moving theater past scenes showing how electricity—and GE appliances—had made life better over the years.

The last of the Disney shows for the fair, It's a Small World, is the only one that has been re-created in each of the company's theme parks. The ride almost never came to be, for by the time sponsor Pepsi-Cola approached Disney, there was less than a year before the fair opened. Since most of the design staff was well immersed in work for the General Electric, Ford, and Illinois pavilions, everyone thought that Disney would turn Pepsi down flat. Instead, he called staff members together for the surprise announcement that they would be taking on the project.

Disney's successes at the fair gained him enormous publicity, and there was even talk of trying to keep a scaled-down version of the fair open after 1965 if he would agree to run it. However, Disney had already set his sights on Florida, and without him, the campaign ended and New York lost its fair.

Occupying an impressive seven-acre site that paralleled Grand Central Parkway, the Ford Pavilion was designed by famed architect Welton Becket. One of the largest pavilions at the fair, the $30 million structure featured a trip back to the days of the dinosaurs, with life-sized re-creations by Walt Disney. The pavilion also included Space City, Ford's prediction of the future, and displays of the company's latest products and prototypes.

Ringed by 100-foot-tall pylons, the Wonder Rotunda greeted visitors as they began their trip back in time. Guests traveled outside the building through the glass-enclosed tunnels of the Magic Skyway aboard one of 160 convertibles powered by an innovative Disney-designed system that is still in use at Disney's theme parks today.

Although at first glance this display looked like regular musical instruments, the Auto Parts Harmonic Orchestra was actually comprised entirely of real car and truck parts. Guests waiting in line were entertained by a medley of songs played by the robotic orchestra. After the New York fair ended, the orchestra was seen at HemisFair '68 in San Antonio, Texas.

Crowds waiting for the Magic Skyway could pass the time looking at the International Gardens, where miniature townscapes represented the countries in which Ford did business. The tiny buildings, streets, and parklands were built on the scale of one-half inch to the foot. It took 20 artists more than 28,000 hours to construct the International Gardens.

Just before guests left the Wonder Rotunda to board their waiting convertibles, they passed a display of new Ford cars, tantalizingly out of reach above an indoor pool complete with fountains. Prominently displayed in a place of honor was the wildly popular Ford Mustang, which made its debut at the fair.

Moving ramps on either side of the Wonder Rotunda led up to the boarding area, passing first through the 145-foot-long Mural Wall. Ahead was a simulated trip through time and then, what everyone was waiting for, Walt Disney's visit to the days of the dinosaurs.

"This is Walt Disney speaking. I'll be riding along to point out some of the things you're going to see from your front-row seat in Mr. Ford's automobiles. Thanks to some old-fashioned magic we call 'imagination,' this Ford Motor Company car will be your time machine for your journey. Carrying you far back in time to the dawn of life on land and transporting you far out into the future." —Magic Skyway narration, 1965.

A family of brontosaurus, calmly enjoying a meal of plants, opened the show in spectacular fashion. The giant figures towered high above the guests passing by in their convertibles, with eerie sounds of a prehistoric world echoing all around.

Two proud triceratops watch their babies break out of the eggs. Guests could choose from a variety of languages for the attraction's soundtrack just by pushing a button on the car's radio. Many young visitors loved switching between the different languages—so much so that the radios needed constant maintenance.

The mighty dinosaurs eventually gave way to new species, including early man. Life was not easy for these newcomers, who had to face attacks from others who wanted to share their primitive homes. Here we see how the need for urgent communication would help spur the development of early languages.

Early man developed tools, such as the spears seen here being used against a trapped woolly mammoth, and the knowledge of how to make fire. Civilization started to advance as these skills were shared among families and friends.

"There's a fellow we would all like to meet! The inventor of the first wheel. As you can see it was a 'trial and error' process: Square wheels. Oblongs. And finally, the round wheel. The wheel gave man a new freedom. Now he could leave the caves behind and travel on to seek his fortune in the wide, wide world." —Magic Skyway narration, 1965.

"We've come a long way in our journey with man. And here we are, on the threshold of tomorrow. Man's achievements in science and industry have carried us here. And like the blast-off of a space vehicle for the moon and beyond, man's achievements have challenged our hopes and rocketed our dreams beyond the horizon." —Magic Skyway narration, 1965.

Added to bring some color and style to the otherwise bland building that housed It's a Small World, the Tower of the Four Winds was a fanciful collection of dozens of mobiles, all powered solely by the wind. More than $200,000 was spent to create the 100-ton structure, which remains one of the largest kinetic sculptures ever created.

Snow White and other Disney characters wave to the crowd below from the Tower of the Four Winds. Behind them is a lounge, and downstairs is a snack bar dispensing Pepsi products. Standing a full 10 stories tall, the tower instantly became one of the most recognizable landmarks at the fair.

Mary Blair was the main designer behind It's a Small World. Disney's salute to UNICEF featured a stylized world of dolls depicting children from around the world, as well as their toys and local settings. The famous (some say infamous) theme song of the same name, written by Richard and Robert Sherman, was sung in many languages throughout the ride.

The late start on designing It's a Small World meant that there was little advance publicity for it. However, early audiences at the fair were captivated by the show, and long lines were the norm for the run of the fair. After the fair ended, the original dolls and props were moved to Disneyland, where they can still be seen today.

The one element of the fair show that did not make the trip to Disneyland was the Tower of the Four Winds. Constructed to survive the possibility of a hurricane in New York, the tower was deemed too heavy to be transported to California. Rumors persist that it was cut into pieces and dumped in a nearby river.

General Electric's Progressland hosted Disney's Carousel of Progress, in which guests stayed seated as the auditorium rotated to the next scene in a show about the marvels of electricity. Afterward, guests could see a live demonstration of nuclear fusion, as well as the latest in General Electric appliances.

One of the most popular shows at the fair, the General Electric pavilion attracted huge crowds that quickly overran its holding area. Despite waiting times of several hours in the brutal New York sun, guests continued to line up for the Carousel of Progress. Happily, a covered waiting area was added in 1965.

The Carousel of Progress featured life in the 1880s, 1920s, 1940s, and present day through a visit with a family enjoying the wonders of electricity. The father hosted each scene and commented on the latest inventions, as members of his family demonstrated them for the audience. All of the actors were robotic figures that featured Disney's new Audio-Animatronic technology—even the family dog, who kept a wary eye on the audience.

As wonderful as things were in each of the decades visited, audiences were reminded that with the help of General Electric scientists, "There's a Great Big Beautiful Tomorrow." That catchy theme song was written by Richard and Robert Sherman, who also wrote the Academy Award–winning songs for Disney's 1964 hit movie *Mary Poppins*.

Mother, who had been working in the kitchen or doing laundry in the earlier scenes, was freed of these chores by her appliances and joined father center stage for the finale. The rest of the family joined in as well, with optimistic predictions that even more leisure time awaited the audience in the years to come—thanks, of course, to the scientists of General Electric.

The roof of the General Electric Pavilion featured a swirling pattern of colored lights, controlled by an early computer system. Sadly, this unique system was not used when the pavilion was later rebuilt at Disneyland.

49

The state of Illinois saluted one of its most famous citizens with a tribute to Abraham Lincoln. The pavilion displayed Lincoln memorabilia, including a draft of the Gettysburg Address in Lincoln's own handwriting, rare photographs, and other historical items. Other exhibits focused on life in Illinois today and the benefits it offered tourists and business.

The high point of the Illinois Pavilion was Disney's Great Moments with Mr. Lincoln, which combined parts of several different speeches by Lincoln into a stirring and patriotic moment backed by inspirational music. The new invention of Audio-Animatronics had audiences gasping in surprise when the robotic Lincoln rose from his chair and began to speak. The show was so successful that a second Lincoln figure was quickly built and added to Disneyland.

Six

POPULUXE AND POP ART

Googie Architecture was born of the post World War II car culture and thrived in the 1950s and 1960s. Bold angles, colorful signs, plate glass, sweeping cantilevered roofs and pop-culture imagery captured the attention of drivers on adjacent streets. Bowling alleys looked like Tomorrowland. Coffee shops looked like something in a Jetsons cartoon.

—Chris Jepsen, *Googie Architecture Online*

The fair offered the greatest concentration of space-age architecture ever assembled. Today, historians call this type of design Googie, a term taken from the design of a Googies Coffee Shop in Los Angeles. According to Chris Jepsen, assistant archivist for the county of Orange (California), it is a style characterized by upswept roofs, concrete domes, exposed steel beams and flying saucer shapes. Googie design has also been known as Populuxe, Jet-Age, Space-Age, and Chinese Modern.

Initially, a design committee proposed that the New York World's Fair construct a huge doughnut-shaped pavilion to house all of the exhibits of the fair. Exhibitors would rent a slice of the doughnut to display their wares. Fair president Robert Moses rejected this idea outright, much to the dismay of the design committee. Moses felt that exhibitors should be allowed to put up whatever structure they deemed appropriate since they were paying to participate in the fair. Adamant about the Fair Corporation itself spending as little money as possible on construction, Moses declared that the doughnut pavilion was out of the question.

The result was that the fairgrounds became a glorious hodgepodge of shapes and designs. The fair was a showcase for some of the greatest names in architecture of the time. Philip Johnson, Eero Saarinen, and Walter Dorwin Teague, among others, contributed pavilion designs for the New York World's Fair. Travelers Insurance built its pavilion in the shape of the company's red umbrella symbol. United States Rubber hosted an 80-foot-tall Ferris wheel in the shape of a tire. On one end of the fairgrounds was an entire 18th-century Flemish village, and on the other end, a 15-story tablelike building that had a roof on which helicopters landed. Chrysler Corporation put together the pop-art extravaganza called Autofare.

Everywhere, it seemed, the future had soared in. Space-age materials and new engineering discoveries allowed designers to construct buildings in shapes and forms never possible before. For the public entering the fairgrounds, it was like walking out of today and into tomorrow.

The Brass Rail Food Service Organization operated many refreshment and souvenir centers throughout the fairgrounds. Utilizing state-of-the-art construction, the roofs of the concession stands were made of air-filled fiberglass cloth and resembled a huge cluster of marshmallows or balloons floating over the patrons. Their award-winning design made them easy to spot from anywhere on the fairgrounds.

Towers, everywhere there were towers. The Seven-Up Pavilion's tower featured a giant clock so that visitors would know when it was time for "the Pause that Refreshes." The tower of the Coca-Cola Pavilion, appearing in the background, contained a carillon. There were observation towers, the Tower of the Four Winds, Flemish bell towers, and even a Column of Jarash—an ancient Roman column displayed at the Jordan Pavilion.

One of the innovations of the space age was a space-frame design that allowed for the construction of geodesic domes. The Pavilion was such a structure and was built by the World's Fair Corporation as an assembly hall and indoor arena. Buckminster Fuller, known as "the father of geodesic domes," went on to design the famous 20-story-high, bubble-shaped geodesic pavilion of the United States for Montreal's Expo '67.

The scalloped concrete roof of the Moody Bible Institute's Sermons from Science exhibit gave this pavilion its most striking feature. The exhibits inside were no less space-age and included a man passing one million volts of electricity through his body in a demonstration meant to convey how faith and knowledge can act in harmony.

Built to resemble a large open garden with two treelike columns and a parasol roof, the Gas Companies Pavilion was an unmistakable landmark, both day and night. In the foreground stands one of 11 Archways of Communication, presented by General Foods and located in various areas around the fairgrounds. These 60-foot-tall arches contained mounted panels that displayed fair information, news, and announcements of public interest.

At the Gas Companies Pavilion was a display of Norge appliances of the future, including the Dishmaker. The Dishmaker made dishes on the spot from large sheets of plastic that loaded at the bottom of the unit and then traveled up the back where gas burners softened and molded them into the desired type of utensil. Instead of washing dirty dishes, simply dispose of them. Potential landfill problems were not addressed.

Large windows formed the Glass Tower of the Pavilion of American Interiors. The pavilion featured the exhibits of more than 120 top furniture and accessories manufacturers. The International Silver Company displayed a Moon Room in which the tea sets and silverware seemed to float in space. Elsewhere, Naugahyde, see-through drapes, bathroom carpeting, and kitchen canister sets "alive" in colors of yellow, olive, blue, and orange tones were on display.

At first glance, the Travelers Insurance Pavilion resembled a futuristic spaceship. The pop art design incorporated Travelers' famous "Red Umbrella of Protection" logo in the top of the pavilion, which was constructed like a red umbrella. Inside, Travelers presented the Triumph of Man, in which life-sized dioramas depicted major challenges and calamities that mankind has overcome during recorded time.

The roof of the Eastman Kodak Pavilion was a fairyland of domes, pinnacles, and curves. Called the Moon Deck, the rooftop afforded excellent views and photo opportunities. The domed structure in the middle of the roof was actually a theater in which the Eastman Chemical Division presented a film about the atom. Looming over the entire pavilion was the Kodak Picture Tower, which looked much like Kodak's then new Carousel slide projectors.

The undulating Moon Deck roof was constructed of reinforced concrete, 363 feet in length. It was supported by an unusual arrangement of columns that, from a distance, made the roof appear to float. Beneath the Moon Deck were displays of Kodak products for photography, X-rays, and movie making.

Kodak's Moon Deck spires were specially designed to provide a unique backdrop for picture taking. While strolling around the Moon Deck, visitors often encountered Emmett Kelly Jr. The world-famous clown made frequent guest appearances at the Kodak pavilion.

The most eye-catching feature of the Kodak pavilion was its 80-foot-tall Picture Tower. Five color prints, each 30 by 36 feet in size, were illuminated day and night. The prints were changed every three or four weeks. Below the tower was a theater where the award-winning Saul Bass film *The Searching Eye* played to overflow audiences.

The lights illuminating the Picture Tower's giant prints threw a total of 15-million candlepower on the photographs. Outriggers at the base of the prints contained a new kind of lamp that was so brilliant that the prints resembled glowing transparencies even when the sun was shining directly on them. The lighting was turned down in the evening when the lamps no longer had to outshine the sun.

Philip Johnson's design for the New York State Pavilion was hailed as one of the architectural masterpieces of the fair. Sixteen 98-foot-tall concrete columns supported the world's largest suspension roof, creating the Tent of Tomorrow. Next door stood three observation towers. Completing the complex was a theater-in-the-round in which a 360-degree motion picture gave visitors a filmed tour of the attractions of the fair's host state.

Conceived as "the County Fair of the Future," the Tent of Tomorrow combined the activity and excitement of a traditional local fair with a dramatic and unique architectural design that envisioned a world of tomorrow. Besides displays of state significance, the pavilion was host to countless high school band concerts and programs showcasing the talents of many New Yorkers.

The most striking feature of the New York State Pavilion was its roof of translucent panels. Resembling stained-glass blocks, the panels allowed sunlight to stream in by day and were lighted from above at night. Occupying almost the entire floor was a 130- by 166-foot terrazzo replica of a Texaco road map of the state. The giant map became one of the best-remembered displays of the fair.

Topping out at 212 feet, the pavilion's observation towers were the tallest structures at the fair. Sky-Streak elevators whisked fairgoers up the exterior of the columns to circular platforms for a sweeping view of the fairgrounds, Long Island, and a distant Manhattan skyline. The height of the towers was dictated by the fair's proximity to LaGuardia Airport. The lowest platform was actually a lounge available for use by visiting dignitaries.

The Paris Exposition of 1889 produced the Eiffel Tower. The Space Needle was constructed for the Seattle World's Fair in 1962. Although no longer in use, the Tent of Tomorrow and the observation towers are still standing in Flushing Meadows–Corona Park. A well-known local landmark, they have gained fame as the setting for several major motion pictures such as Men in Black and The Wiz.

60

Johnson's Wax presented the Francis Thompson film *To Be Alive!* in a pavilion resembling a flying saucer spaceport. The Academy Award–winning 12-minute movie was the film highlight of the fair, illustrating the simple joys of being alive the world over. After the fair closed, the Golden Rondelle was reconstructed at the Racine, Wisconsin, headquarters of Johnson's Wax, and the film entertained visitors there for another 30 years.

The Port Authority of New York and New Jersey was responsible for securing exhibitors for the Transportation Area of the fair, and appropriately, that pavilion took the shape of a giant T looming over the fairgrounds. This design was quite practical as the pavilion served as the aerial gateway to the fair, with helicopters arriving and departing for area airports from its rooftop.

A Sikorsky helicopter of New York Airways arrives on the rooftop heliport of the Port Authority building. The pavilion featured one of the fair's most exclusive restaurants. Just below rooftop level, the Top of the Fair offered fine dining with a magnificent view. A 360-degree movie about the Port Authority of New York and New Jersey was shown in the circular structure at the base of the table-topped pavilion.

One of displays at the heliport was a model of the Port Authority's World Trade Center. Ground was broken for this lower Manhattan office complex in 1966, just one year after the fair closed. It is ironic, in light of the fair's theme of Peace through Understanding, that the World Trade Center was destroyed in a terrorist attack just 35 years later.

By day, the Electric Companies Tower of Light reflected sunlight off hundreds of aluminum-covered prisms. By night, the panels were lighted in pastel colors, creating one of the fair's most striking visual effects. From the center shown the world's brightest searchlight: a 12-billion-candlepower beam. A few years later, energy shortages made such an extravagant display seem excessive. In the space age, energy was inexpensive and plentiful.

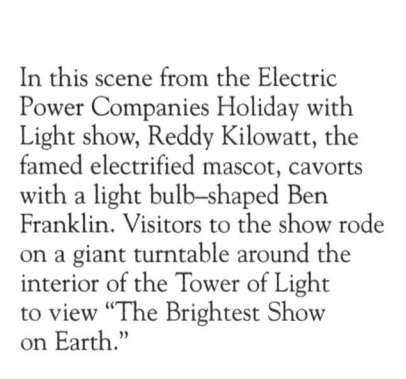

In this scene from the Electric Power Companies Holiday with Light show, Reddy Kilowatt, the famed electrified mascot, cavorts with a light bulb–shaped Ben Franklin. Visitors to the show rode on a giant turntable around the interior of the Tower of Light to view "The Brightest Show on Earth."

63

Chrysler Corporation, realizing that it would be unable to compete against the millions of dollars being spent by its rivals, steered clear of technical gimmickry and gave its exhibit a fanciful tone. The display included a giant engine and automobile, the Bil Baird Marionettes, and a zoo of animals constructed of auto parts.

Called Autofare, the Chrysler exhibit was a pop art extravaganza. More than 1,000 umbrella-shaded chairs for weary fairgoers surrounded the perimeter of five islands set in an oval-shaped man-made lake. Spraying fountains framed Chrysler automobiles that seemed to float on water jets. Inside Chrysler's giant engine, a writhing 50-foot-long dragon drove three 8-foot-high pistons in a whimsical display of mechanical might.

A 10-story rocket with engines spraying water symbolized Chrysler's role in America's space and missile efforts. Elsewhere, in Chrysler's Pentastar Theater, Carby Carburetor and his friends, creations of the famed Bil Baird Marionettes, performed in a musical production called Show-Go-Round, which was set on a giant revolving stage.

Car bodies transported fairgoers through a simulated Chrysler auto production line. Riders passed through an area of mechanical workmen and giant quality control gauges in a pop art display of the manufacture of automobiles.

Autofare's giant automobile was nearly 80 feet long and 50 feet wide, with wheels that were nearly two stories tall. The underside of the car sat eight feet off the ground so that fairgoers could walk beneath it. The massive structure actually contained a lounge for important visitors.

Perhaps the best known pop art entry at the fair was United States Rubber's giant tire Ferris wheel. Towering 80 feet high, the big tire was an easily recognizable symbol of the fair and a runaway hit for its corporate sponsor. After the fair, the tire was dismantled and moved to Detroit, where it remains today as a Uniroyal advertising display along a Motor City expressway—sadly, without the Ferris wheel.

Seven

COLD WARFAIR

*But unless we can achieve the theme of this Fair,
"Peace Through Understanding;" . . . our hopes of today, these
proud achievements, will go under in the devastation of tomorrow.*

—Pres. Lyndon B. Johnson,
opening the New York World's Fair,
April 22, 1964

The theme show at the 1962 Seattle World's Fair had been an attraction titled Century 21: The Threshold and the Threat. As the 1964–1965 New York World's Fair opened, the free and totalitarian worlds were embroiled in a conflict that none hoped would ever manifest itself in actual war, for it would surely end in worldwide nuclear holocaust. If the space age was the threshold to a future of limitless promise, then the cold war was the threat that mankind would never survive to see the future.

Because the fair was conceived, planned, and constructed during the late 1950s and early 1960s, world events of that period had a direct bearing on what the fairgoer saw. For a time it looked as though the Soviet Union would accept an invitation to participate. A site had been selected for its pavilion, but negotiations faltered and the Russians did not exhibit at the fair. The China pavilion was sponsored by Taiwan, not Peking, since the Communist government of mainland China was not recognized by America as the official government of China. The Underground Home showed the benefits of underground living, including protection from nuclear fallout. The heavy influence of industry at the fair was very much by design, stressing the benefits of economic freedom resulting from a capitalist economy.

The theme of the United States Pavilion was Challenge to Greatness. It had been endorsed by the late Pres. John F. Kennedy and reflected Pres. Lyndon B. Johnson's Great Society initiatives. The U.S. Space Park was filled with a display of spacecraft with names like *Freedom 7* and *Liberty Bell 7*. At the Hall of Free Enterprise, exhibits showed the superiority of the economic principles on which a democratic system of free enterprise rests.

The cold war outlasted both the fair and the space age. A North Vietnamese attack on a U.S. Navy destroyer in the Gulf of Tonkin in August 1964 brought a U.S. bombing retaliation, which marked the beginning of major American involvement in Vietnam. This cold war incident, and the tumultuous decade that followed it, erased forever the blind optimism of the space age.

The Pennsylvania exhibit first appeared at the fair in June 1965 and was paid for entirely by private donations from Pennsylvanians. The only attraction on display at the pavilion was a full-sized replica of the Liberty Bell from Independence Hall in Philadelphia. The express purpose of the exhibit was to emphasize "liberty, freedom and democracy."

The German city of Berlin chose a site symbolically situated across the street from the United States Pavilion to emphasize the close ties between Americans and Berliners. The pavilion presented a look at the culture and industry of a city whose citizens lived their lives "in the shadow of Communism," according to the fair's *Official Guidebook*. One of the fair's two-passenger Escorter vehicles, a space-age rickshaw of sorts, passes by.

Flags of many nations wave in front of the United Nations Pavilion. The pavilion was sponsored for 1965 by the International Exhibit on the United Nations Inc., a New York membership corporation dedicated to furthering an understanding of the aims and accomplishments of the United Nations. It occupied the building originally constructed by the African nation of Sierra Leone.

Continental Insurance presented a filmed cartoon tribute to some of the unsung heroes of the American Revolution. Patriots Henry Knox, Timothy Murphy, Deborah Sampson, and others were saluted in a show called *Cinema '76*. The pavilion formed a shadowbox so that the film could be viewed from an outdoor platform in full daylight. Revolutionary War artifacts were displayed inside.

The federal government appropriated $17 million for the United States Pavilion and exhibit. The pavilion was the largest cantilevered building ever constructed, with 150,000 square feet of exhibit space raised on four columns. Measuring 330 feet on each side and rising 84 feet above the ground, the massive building was brought down to human scale by use of a new type of translucent glass wall designed for the exterior.

Four supporting columns set back from the edges of the pavilion made the entire structure seem to float 20 feet above the ground. In the center of the building, a gracefully rising pyramid of steps led through landscaping and waterfalls up to a colorful open Garden Court at the second level. Here, there was access to all exhibit areas amid an atmosphere of peaceful relief from the bustle of the fair.

Pres. John F. Kennedy had championed the fair and the United States Pavilion with its theme of Challenge to Greatness. He had broken ground for the structure in December 1962. His assassination, 11 months later, cast a pall over the country and the upcoming opening of the fair just months away. A bust of his likeness, on display at the lower main entrance to the pavilion, served as a memorial to the slain president.

Challenges to Freedom was one issue facing the country in the 1960s. The United States Pavilion sought to provide an accurate and meaningful look at the character of a nation serving as a model for freedom. The featured show was a ride called the American Journey, in which 55-seat moving grandstands passed 110 movie screens of varied sizes and shapes that displayed a capsulated film history of America.

Freedom of the Human Spirit is silhouetted against the lighted facade of the United States Pavilion. The exterior walls of the pavilion were constructed of thousands of multicolored panels. At night, reflector lights placed inside the walls gave the structure a sparkling appearance. The United States Pavilion was retained after the close of the fair. However, no use was ever found for the structure, and it was demolished in 1977.

Nuclear bombs were not the only explosions causing concern in the space age. The population explosion was on the public's mind as it looked to the future. The Equitable Life Assurance Society Pavilion presented a remarkable display on population in the Demograph, a 44-foot-long tabulator that displayed an up-to-the-minute estimate of the U.S. population. Beneath the Demograph, colored displays and maps explained shifting population trends throughout the country.

Eight

A WORLD'S FAIR?

The B.I.E. attempted to "outlaw" the 1964–1965 Fair but did not succeed.

—Robert Moses, New York World's Fair 1964–1965,
Corporation president, January 24, 1963

In 1961, Robert Moses journeyed to Paris to seek approval from the Bureau of International Expositions (BIE) to host a world's fair in New York. The bureau regulates world's fairs and sets ground rules for cities wishing to host them. The United States, not a member of the bureau, sought its official blessing to ensure participation in the fair by nations who were members.

In the United States, unlike in many other countries, public monies do not directly fund expositions. To make sure that the fair was adequately funded and to have a surplus to repay the investors and build a post-fair park, the World's Fair Corporation decided to hold its show for two years and to charge exhibitors rent for the sites. These seemingly practical decisions led to a confrontation with the BIE, whose regulations state that a world's fair may be held for no more than a six-month period and that exhibitors must be allowed to participate rent free.

When the BIE balked at New York's bid, Moses publicly attacked the organization. Perhaps more diplomacy on the part of the World's Fair Corporation and less intransigence on the part of the bureau could have resulted in a compromise. Reportedly stung by the public attack, the BIE denied New York's bid for its fair and formally invoked a rule that their participatory nations could not exhibit at fairs hosted by nonmember countries. This boycott resulted in the loss of participation by Great Britain, Canada, and France, among other major industrialized nations. Cold war politics led to a different kind of boycott, as the Soviet Union and aligned nations also turned their backs on New York's fair.

Undaunted by the BIE ban, the fair turned to trade organizations within some of the boycotting nations to stage quasi-official participation. Other countries simply ignored the ban, and no fewer than 46 international pavilions were eventually constructed. The loss of major international displays meant that smaller countries, whose exhibits would have been lost among those of larger nations, were able to present well-attended shows. The 1964–1965 New York World's Fair will forever be known as the only world's fair in modern history that was not an official world's fair.

By far, the most popular international exhibit was the Vatican Pavilion. The elegant oval pavilion, topped by a golden-roofed chapel, exhibited scores of priceless works of art. Chief among them was the fair's most valuable and inspiring work, Michelangelo's sculpture *Pieta*. The Astral Fountain's column of water spray rising within a revolving birdcage-like structure of golden stars appears in the foreground.

The *Pieta* depicts the crucified Christ in the arms of his mother. Only General Motors' Futurama ride drew more attendance during the fair's two six-month seasons. In October 1965, Pope Paul VI visited the pavilion and viewed Michelangelo's sculpture in its world's fair setting during his historic trip to the United Nations. His visit marked the first time a pope had traveled to the United States.

74

The island nations of Polynesia were represented at the fair in an attractive pavilion constructed to resemble a South Seas island longhouse. In a lagoon located in the front courtyard, Polynesian representatives gave demonstrations of piloting outrigger canoes and diving for oysters.

The main feature of the Philippine Pavilion was a raised restaurant built in the shape of a *salakot*, the traditional wide-brimmed hat worn throughout the Philippines to provide protection from the sun. Elaborate wood-carved panels depicted the story of the islands.

The Indonesian Pavilion, one of the largest International Area pavilions constructed for the fair, showed life on the islands of Java, Bali, and Sumatra. In 1965, anti-American sentiment caused Indonesia's President Sukarno to withdraw his country's participation in the fair. The pavilion was subsequently closed, fenced off, and patrolled by security guards during the second season. It was dismantled and shipped to Jakarta following the close of the fair.

The ornate and interesting design of the Hong Kong Pavilion, which included replicas of three Chinese junk sailing ships outside, drew crowds to what was merely a large shopping bazaar and restaurant.

Mexico was represented at the fair by an architecturally elegant pavilion. A huge domed skylight allowed natural light to filter into the interior of the raised structure. Exhibits highlighted Mexican history and art, and frequent outdoor performances by aerial acrobats and dancers entertained passersby.

The Republic of China Pavilion represented the people of Taiwan because America did not formally recognize the Communist government of mainland China. The pavilion was an opulent red and gold re-creation of an imperial palace. All of the components of the pavilion, except for the structural steel, were handmade in Taiwan and shipped to the fair for reassembly.

Visitors to the Greek Pavilion were welcomed by a 120-foot-long frieze of men and chariots on parade above a doorway reminiscent of ancient Greek architecture. Inside, displays told the story of ancient and modern Greece.

A children's playground with a Tivoli-like atmosphere allowed parents to leave their fair-weary children in an attended area while they explored the Danish Pavilion's attractions. The exhibit's theme was Meet the Danes, and visitors were able to explore displays about Hans Christian Andersen and Niels Bohr. Shops sold Danish dinnerware, glassware, and furniture.

The government of Sweden was able to get around the Bureau of International Expositions' ban by simply creating a corporation and exhibiting under its auspices. This attractive pavilion of blue and gold was meant to represent a stylized ship in recognition of the country's great seafaring heritage.

Egypt, one of the members of the United Arab Republic, had an official representation at the fair. Ancient Egyptian artifacts, including those of King Tutankhamen, were on display. A major exhibit was given over to the international project under way to raise the temples of Ramses II and Queen Nefertari high above the rising waters caused by the construction of the Aswan High Dam.

India's Indira Ghandi was among the honored guests who opened the world's fair on April 22, 1964. India had a major official government-sponsored presence at the fair. Displays showed how industry and education had flourished under India's democracy. The nation of 450 million people presented a major exhibition on ancient and modern artwork that reflected its long history and culture.

Constructed of wood and steel, the Austrian Pavilion resembled an Alpine ski lodge. After the fair closed, the pavilion was dismantled and moved to the Cockaigne ski area in Cherry Valley, just east and north of Jamestown, New York. The pavilion remains there today, looking very much as it did at the world's fair.

Traditional Islamic architecture graced the Sudanese Pavilion. Sudan was among several emerging nations who found it a matter of great national pride to be represented alongside the established nations exhibiting at the New York World's Fair. Displays included relics from the Nubian civilization, which flourished in the Sudan area some 4,000 years earlier.

The Kingdom of Jordan constructed a contemporary space-age pavilion. Displays included an ancient Roman ruin called the Column of Jarash. Presented as a gift to the city of New York by Jordan following the fair, the ruin remains on display in Flushing Meadows–Corona Park today. Controversy broke out over a mural on display that depicted the plight of the Palestinian people. The mural asked, "Won't you help?"

A total of 24 African nations including the Congo, Kenya, Ethiopia, Rwanda, and Somalia were represented in a pavilion constructed to resemble a village of African huts on stilts. A filmed presentation gave highlights of the participating countries. Elsewhere, a veritable zoo of African animals delighted visitors.

The huts of the African Pavilion, traditional in design, were constructed of plastic and wood and were meant to suggest Africa's modern outlook.

The Korean Pavilion was a strikingly modern design. The pavilion displayed ancient artifacts, silks, and folk dancing. It also offered a slide and film show that gave fairgoers an idea of what life was like in the modern-day republic of Korea, as it recovered from the decade-old conflict with North Korea.

The Spanish Pavilion was hailed as the architectural masterpiece of the fair. Spain ignored the Bureau of International Expositions' boycott and presented a remarkable exhibition. The exhibits included priceless works of art by El Greco, Goya, and Velazquez. Other displays showed modern Spain and the Spain of history and legend. The pavilion was reassembled in St. Louis following the fair and is now part of that city's Pavilion Hotel.

A bed of blooming geraniums fronts the pavilions of Japan and Austria. The exterior wall of the Japanese pavilion was constructed with lava stones shipped from Japan and reassembled at the fair by expert Japanese craftsmen. A second, more contemporary pavilion housed displays of modern Japanese industry.

One of the most ornately designed pavilions at the fair was that of Thailand. Built to resemble a traditional Buddhist shrine, the pavilion displayed ancient Thai artifacts and the arts, crafts, and industrial products of modern-day Thailand. Following the fair, the pavilion was dismantled and shipped to Montreal, where it was reassembled as the Thailand Pavilion for Expo '67.

Nine

SOMETHING FOR EVERYBODY

A Fair . . . must indeed have a worthy theme and central purpose but there must also be something exciting in it for everybody.

—Robert Moses, New York World's Fair 1964–1965, Corporation president, September 12, 1962

Robert Moses believed in allowing great freedom in what exhibitors could present. Although science and the space age were favorite topics, other participants looked to more traditional displays. Some attempted to tie the fair's unifying theme of Peace through Understanding in with their exhibits; others simply presented a show that would sell whatever they hoped to sell. That exhibits were commercial in nature can partially be blamed on the Bureau of International Expositions boycott, since most international exhibits were sponsored by trade organizations interested in selling the products of their countries. Many state governments were unwilling to appropriate tax dollars to host exhibits, and thus, the fair had to look to state commerce organizations for participation. Corporate exhibitors often presented their message in a show in which fairgoers viewed the products in the soft-sell of highly imaginative and costly presentations.

The press was harsh on the fair, criticizing the exposition's overly commercial displays, theme, and architecture. Whether the continuous negative press had an effect on the attendance is unknown. It was projected that the exposition would ultimately attract 70 million visitors, and the fair spent accordingly. When only 27 million attended in 1964, it soon became obvious that the fair would run into financial difficulties, and it did. Almost two million fewer visitors attended the second season, and charges of gross mismanagement hung heavily over the World's Fair Corporation. Investors were eventually repaid 62.4¢ on the dollar. The World's Fair Corporation elected to pour the fair's cash assets back into the restoration of Flushing Meadows–Corona Park rather than fulfill its debt obligations.

Criticism of the fair amounted to little in the minds of visitors who had a wonderland of attractions to keep them entertained. Rocket displays were just a few steps away from life-sized dinosaurs. Visitors could start their day at the IBM Pavilion, learning how computers make decisions, and then head over to the Pepsi Pavilion for a Walt Disney–created salute to the UNICEF organization. Before heading home, they could gaze in quiet wonder at Michelangelo's 500-year-old *Pieta* sculpture at the Vatican Pavilion and end their day of adventure at the Hell Drivers auto racetrack. The 1964–1965 New York World's Fair was truly something for everyone.

The Big Sky Country echoed Montana's state motto. In Montana's exhibit at the fair, seven railroad cars contained displays that included the works of two of the West's most famous artists: Charles M. Russell and Frederic Remington. The beat of drums was heard as part of a presentation of tribal dancing given by Native Americans encamped at the exhibit.

Wisconsin displayed a 17.5-ton cheddar that was billed as "the World's Largest Cheese." The pavilion's rotunda, in the shape of a stylized yellow Indian tepee, survived the fair's wreckers and is now home to Central Wisconsin Broadcasting and WCCN Radio in the west-central Wisconsin town of Neillsville. The building looks just as it did at the fair and hosts a gift shop selling "the World's Fairest Gifts."

The New York World's Fair gave neighboring state New Jersey the perfect party with which to celebrate its tercentenary. The pavilion itself won an award for outstanding architecture, which included soaring masts that supported 21 suspended, peaked-roof exhibit buildings.

Among New Jersey's displays were models of the Telstar and Relay II communications satellites and the Tiros weather satellite which all were constructed in the state. With so many visitors coming to the fair from New Jersey, the pavilion hosted one of the major U.S. state displays.

From Drumbeat to Telstar was the theme of the Bell Telephone System presentation. The pavilion consisted of an upper floating wing, with a multimedia ride through the history of communications. Lower-level exhibits included the famous Picturephones, which made their debut at the fair. Visitors spoke with characters in Disneyland on telephones displaying a live picture of the person—or mouse—on the other end of the line.

The raised wing of the Bell Pavilion dwarfs one of the fair's Glide-a-Ride trains as it passes by. The wing itself, which rested on four pylons that made it appear to float over the grounds, was 400 feet long and covered by fiberglass panels. Fairgoers ascended a ramp to a platform to reach the seats on the continuously moving 1,000-chair ride train that journeyed through the communications presentation.

The ride train of the Bell System Pavilion carried fairgoers in comfort past a series of movie presentations about the history of communications, from drumbeat and smoke signals through the first written word and the development of printing and telegraphy to the marvels of telecommunication satellites and international communication network links.

The Sinclair Oil Company went millions of years into the past to present one of the fair's most popular exhibits. Dinoland displayed nine life-sized dinosaur models in an attraction that was designed to show the source of fossil fuels. The largest dinosaur model, the brontosaurus, was 27 feet tall and 70 feet long. His head swung back and forth as he peered down on the motorists traveling along the Grand Central Parkway.

Dinoland's models, such as this Trachodon, towered over fairgoers. The dinosaurs were constructed in upstate New York and shipped fully assembled by barge down the Hudson River to the fair. The sight of nine dinosaurs floating down the Hudson caused a traffic jam in the city, as thousands of motorists stopped their cars on bridges and highways to watch the water procession pass by.

After the fair closed, Dinoland was loaded onto two flatbed trucks and taken on tour around the country. Most of the dinosaur models eventually found homes, some at dinosaur parks in Texas and Utah. Others are on display in Cleveland, Louisville, Milwaukee, and Independence, Kansas, and copies made from the original molds are exhibited elsewhere. The tiny ornitholestes has been lost to history.

The space age brought Americans face-to-face with the computer, and IBM turned to architect Eero Saarinen and designer Charles Eames to develop its remarkable presentation for the fair. Rust-colored, 90-foot-tall steel trees, topped by a translucent green plastic canopy of leaves, formed the Garden of Learning, in which computer-related exhibits were displayed. IBM's main presentation, the Information Machine, was within the white ovoid structure perched atop the metallic garden.

Covered with thousands of the letters I-B-M, the Information Machine was a unique theater in which the similarity between human and computer logic was explained. In preparation to see the film, 500 fairgoers took places on the People Wall, a grandstand-like structure that stood directly beneath the ovoid theater, which was 90 feet above. An IBM host appeared on a small platform in front of them to welcome them to the show.

As the show began, the host ascended from audience view and hydraulic rams pushed the entire grandstand and audience high into the ovoid theater to view the IBM presentation. Charles Eames' film was shown on nine screens that sometimes presented a complete image and at other times individual images. When the 12-minute show ended, the People Wall descended from the theater and the audience disembarked.

In an eerie view resembling a scene from a science fiction movie, the IBM host descended from the Information Machine through the canopied roof of the pavilion. After welcoming the audience, seated on the People Wall, the host ascended back into the theater to narrate the show.

The host's platform was a most unusual elevator that traveled between the Information Machine and the People Wall. It traveled up and down, using a telescoping pole, much like the old power antennas on automobiles.

The host entered and exited the Information Machine on the platform through an opening in the exterior of the ovoid theater. The various pavilions at the fair used many techniques to move audiences through their shows. IBM's People Wall and host elevator were among the most unique.

From high above on the People Wall, visitors were treated to a bird's-eye view of the Industrial Area of the fair. To get to their seat on the wall, fairgoers traversed a mazelike structure of stairways and platforms. Strolling musicians entertained them while they waited for the IBM show to begin.

Other IBM exhibits included the Probability Machine, which explained the law of averages. A computer read handwritten dates and retrieved corresponding headlines from the news of that day. Fairgoers could type postcards on IBM's new Selectric typewriters in which a whirling letter-covered ball replaced the traditional array of strikers. The Selectric's ball was said to have been the inspiration for the design of the pavilion's ovoid theater.

94

Alaska had become the 49th state just five years prior to the opening of the fair. The state's traditional pavilion was constructed in the shape of an igloo, with tall totem poles displayed outdoors. Meanwhile, neighbor Missouri selected displays that tied the state to the aerospace industry of the space age.

Formica, the versatile, decorative surface covering that was the hit of the 1960s, was represented at the fair by the Formica World's Fair House. Perched atop the fairground's only hill, the product's parent company, American Cyanamid, took every opportunity to display household goods and furnishings covered in Formica. Even the children's bedroom walls had a Formica covering. Replica Formica World's Fair Houses were constructed around the country following the fair.

95

Du Pont's pavilion was surrounded by globe lights that resembled interlocking molecules. Inside the building, three theaters played to capacity audiences. In the Blue and Gold Theaters, an original Michael Brown presentation called the Wonderful World of Chemistry had live casts simultaneously performing a Broadway-style musical revue that presented a lively capsule history of Du Pont and its products. The show was presented an astounding 42 times each day.

Fairgoers funneled into Du Pont's Red Theater to see a remarkable demonstration of chemical magic. Displayed were 12 chemical tricks that included this one, in which a piece of cloth had the letters Z-E-P-E-L printed on with the invisible stain repellent Zepel. Liquids of various sorts were then poured on the cloth to stain it completely. The letters stood out since they were stain resistant.

Set on four acres of land, the Beautiful Belgian Village re-created a complete Flemish village of the year 1800. Picturesque Belgium, as it was also called, contained no less than 100 detailed structures, cobblestone streets, a canal and bridge, a village church, and a city hall with a rathskeller under it. The quaint village was a stark contrast to the futuristic pavilions surrounding it.

The Belgian village was the largest international pavilion constructed for the fair. Artisans sold wares from the authentically re-created shops. Collections of Flemish artwork and World War II relics were on display, and an ornate carousel drew large crowds. The exhibit was immensely popular with fairgoers, and even an additional admission charge of $1 over and above the fair's admission proved not to be a deterrent to attracting visitors.

Amidst the space-age atmosphere of the fair, the Liebmann Breweries presented Rheingold's Little Old New York. The pavilion was actually a collection of shops and restaurants featuring Liebmann's Rheingold beer. The quaint 1900s atmosphere of the eatery and pub provided a quiet, peaceful spot to escape from the crowds of the fair.

In another display of make-believe, the Hollywood USA Pavilion brought motion picture–making techniques to fair audiences. The pavilion was constructed behind a facade of Grauman's Chinese Theater, and entertainers performing at the fair were invited to leave behind their hand prints and signatures in the cement sidewalk squares outside the replica Hollywood landmark.

Wax museums seemed to be all the rage in the 1960s, and Walter's International Wax Museum was the fair's version of these rather unusual attractions. At Walter's, fairgoers could view $2 million worth of wax figurines. The collection, which contained 160 figures, was the largest of its kind ever displayed in the United States up to that time.

Ed Sullivan and Paul McCartney appear in wax at Walter's International Wax Museum in the fair's Amusement Area. In 1964, Ed Sullivan introduced the Beatles to American audiences on his weekly television variety show. In 1965, the real "Fab Four" landed at the fair's heliport and were driven by armored car through the fair to their now famous concert at nearby Shea Stadium.

Religion played an important part in the lives of Americans in the 1960s. No less than nine religious-oriented pavilions were constructed for the fair. The Protestant and Orthodox Center's courtyard featured an 80-foot-high tower with a cross surrounded by 34 pylons honoring sectarian religious founders. Elsewhere at the fair, visitors could explore faith at the American-Israel, Christian Science, Russian Orthodox–Greek Catholic, Wycliff Bible Translators, Vatican, and Sermons from Science Pavilions, among others.

The towering facade of the Mormon Pavilion was a re-creation of the famed Mormon Temple in Salt Lake City. A golden statue of the angel Moroni trumpeted from the central tower. The pavilion presented a 15-minute film history of the Mormon faith and displayed various religious artifacts.

One of the most famous evangelists of the 1960s was Rev. Billy Graham, whose stadium-based Crusades were televised worldwide to audiences of millions. The Billy Graham Pavilion at the fair sought to extend his ministry by reaching out to the millions of people who visited the fair. Many fairgoers answered the call after the showing of the pavilion's film presentation of *Man in the 5th Dimension*.

Florida displays included vacation attractions, leisure housing, and space industry–related exhibits. In a separate arena-like building, porpoises and marine life delighted fairgoers with a free show. The most attention-getting feature of the pavilion, however, was the giant plastic orange atop the Florida Citrus Tower. In a booth at the base of the tower, fairgoers were invited to sample fresh squeezed orange juice courtesy of the Florida Citrus Growers Association.

In another departure from space-age themes, the Avis car rental company presented the Avis Antique Car Ride in which anyone 10 years or older could drive authentic open-topped five-eighths-scale antique automobiles down a rustic country lane. Drivers roared past spectators at speeds approaching four miles per hour.

The Coca-Cola Pavilion's theme was World of Refreshment. In the show, visitors were able to experience the sights, sounds, and smells of five world settings including an Alpine lodge and the Taj Mahal. In a move that was somewhat less than soft-sell, bottles of Coca-Cola could easily be spotted in the various world scenes. The tower in the pavilion's courtyard contained a 610-bell carillon. World-famous carillonneurs gave daily free concerts.

A reflection of the times, the General Cigar Company had a major exhibit at the New York World's Fair. Inside the two-story pavilion of glass and steel was a presentation co-sponsored by the magazine *Sports Illustrated* that gave a bird's-eye view of sporting events projected into a well that was set in the floor. Fairgoers actually viewed the event as if they were seated above the action.

Magician Mark Wilson prepares to make his assistant disappear "in a puff of smoke" in his magic show at the General Cigar Hall of Magic. The 10-minute show was presented three times an hour in the pavilion's theater. Outside the pavilion, a machine blew large smoke rings (non-tobacco) high into the air.

New York City presented its exhibit in the building the city constructed for the 1939–1940 New York World's Fair. Between the fairs, the building served as the headquarters for the United Nations in New York while its new headquarters building was being constructed in Manhattan. The building remains in Flushing Meadows–Corona Park and now houses the Queens Museum of Art.

The highlight of New York City's presentation at the fair was an immense model of the city. The model measured 180 by 100 feet, and the buildings were constructed on a scale of 1 inch to 100 feet. Every building in the city's five boroughs was re-created. This incredibly detailed model is still on display at the Queens Museum of Art. It is updated periodically to reflect changes to the city's profile.

RCA's exhibit featured color television, and fairgoers could see themselves on closed-circuit color TV. The pavilion also contained the fair's color television network, complete with studio and production facilities. Broadcasts originating from the pavilion were sent outside the fair and to television monitors situated around the fairgrounds. In a space-age twist, pictures of lost children were also broadcast to sets throughout the fair, hopefully to be spotted by anxious parents.

Something for everyone? Not at the Clairol Pavilion, where only women were allowed. Visitors boarded the Color Carousel for a personalized beauty consultation or peered into round reflecting pods that ringed the front of the pavilion to see how they might look in various hair styles and colors.

A fleet of Hertz strollers waits for riders outside of the General Electric pavilion. These car-shaped strollers, which promoted the slogan "Let Hertz Put You in the Driver's Seat," were so popular that more than 100 of them vanished during the first two weeks of the fair alone.

Who has not wanted his own money tree? A total of $1 million of American and foreign currency was featured in this tree-shaped exhibit at the entrance to the American Express Pavilion. The money was removed between seasons for safekeeping.

Ten

THE BEAT GOES ON

Charleston was once the rage, uh huh
History has turned the page, uh huh
And men still keep on marching off to war
Electrically they keep a baseball score
The beat goes on, the beat goes on.

—Sonny and Cher, Atlantic Records, July 1965

Within hours after the gates closed on October 17, 1965, trucks rolled onto the fairgrounds to begin removing exhibits and dismantling pavilions. Buildings that could not be justified as belonging in a post-fair park were demolished. The residents of neighboring communities who had lived with the fair for years could scarcely believe their eyes as landmark after landmark vanished. On June 3, 1967, Flushing Meadows–Corona Park was turned over to the New York City Parks Department in better condition than when it was leased for $1 to the World's Fair Corporation eight years earlier as the site of the fair.

Scrapbooks contain the carefully preserved collections of mementos that connect today to the events of yesterday. The city of New York had been presented with a kind of scrapbook of the fair. New exhibit halls, a new museum, green spaces, statuary, and fountains were the mementos. At the center of it all stood Unisphere, "reminding succeeding generations of a pageant of surpassing interest and significance." Unfortunately, the fair's scraps were not preserved. Faced with budget woes, the city diverted maintenance funds elsewhere. The park deteriorated. Only after decades of neglect did officials begin to realize the importance of the park and the legacies left behind from two world's fairs. Modern-day caretakers of Flushing Meadows are still working to preserve what remains.

In the 40 years since the fair closed, history has indeed turned many pages. The optimism of the space age crumbled under the weight of Vietnam, energy shortages, ecological concerns, political scandals, race riots, and terrorism. We won the space race and then wondered how we could continue to explore the heavens while there were so many problems on earth. We won the cold war as well but still yearn for "Peace through Understanding" as men keep on marching off to war.

The basic purpose of every world's fair, no matter how lofty the theme, is to educate and entertain. Toward that end, the fair was a resounding success. Millions of people who were fortunate enough to have attended it still look back on it fondly. For many, it was a high point in their lives. Others point to it as the inspiration for lifetime careers in the sciences and the arts. The greatest lesson learned from the fair can best be summed up in the final narration of General Motors' successful Futurama ride. It is as timely today as it was in the space age: "Technology can point the way to a future of limitless promise, but man must chart his own course into tomorrow. A course that frees the mind and the spirit as it improves the well-being of mankind."

Seen here just two years after the fair closed, the once bustling fairgrounds had largely given way to the more tranquil setting of Flushing Meadows–Corona Park. Unfortunately, most of the original plans for the park had to be dropped when the fair ran out of money.

Nevertheless, the park remains an important part of life in Queens, with millions of visitors enjoying the quiet and solitude of this metropolitan oasis—as well as countless picnics, bike rides, and sporting events. Here, a baseball field stands on the former site of the General Motors Pavilion.

Stone benches and a granite memorial mark the site of the Westinghouse time capsules from the two New York World's Fairs. These buried receptacles are not to be opened until the year 6938. One can only wonder what the park, and the world, will look like then.

The New York State Pavilion still stands, but the stranded Sky-Streak elevator has been waiting in vain for passengers for decades. Today, 40 years have passed since the New York World's Fair opened and history has, indeed, turned many pages. How does the fair hold up in light of the passage of nearly a half-century of time? To look back at the fair now is to see it as a punctuation mark at the end of an era.

The cable cars of the Swiss Sky Ride bob gaily over the fairgrounds. The Sky Ride traversed the International Area of the fair from one end to the other. Besides being a quick and economical means of getting from here to there, the ride offered great aerial views of the fair and wonderful picture-taking opportunities.

The view of the fair's Main Mall from high above on the Swiss Sky Ride was a lovely sight. *The Rocket Thrower* fronts the splashing Fountains of the Fairs, while the Bell System "floats" in the distance behind the spraying jets of the Fountain of the Planets. International and industrial pavilions flanked the tree-lined axis.

The traditional architecture of the Hong Kong pavilion stood in sharp contrast to the space-age pavilions of the industrial giants when viewed from the Sky Ride. The ovoid theater of IBM's pavilion and the "floating wing" of the Bell Telephone System were unmistakable landmarks in the distance.

The wooden-peaked front of the Venezuelan Pavilion was one of the sights from the Swiss Sky Ride. Denmark wisely painted "SAS" on the roof of its pavilion, beyond, so that Sky Riders would know that Scandinavian Airlines System was one of the host's of that country's pavilion. The domed roof of the Pavilion, sponsored by the World's Fair Corporation, could be seen in the distance.

111

A favorite view from the fair's high point, the 212-foot towers of the New York State Pavilion, always included the Unisphere surrounded by the Fountains of the Continents. The square-shaped United States Pavilion and Shea Stadium stood in the background. Beyond them, Constellations and brand new Boeing 727 jets roared off the runways of LaGuardia Airport.

It is difficult to believe that the glorious collage of buildings, with their competing shapes, sizes, and designs, could all come crashing down in just a matter of months to be replaced by grass, shrubs, and seedlings, but that is just what happened. The fair was never meant to be permanent. Everything was designed and constructed to benefit the park that would follow the fair.

The arterial highways that surrounded the fair were created or vastly improved in order to accommodate the number of visitors expected to travel them. Taking highway construction into account, it cost over $1 billion to create the fair at Flushing Meadows. Much of the money that went into site preparation benefited the city and park after the fair ended.

The Beautiful Belgian Village did not open until late in the summer of 1964, well into the fair's first season. Despite its beauty, it was only temporary and was demolished along with the rest of the fair during the winter of 1966. Today, a marble bench marks the site of the nearby oval-shaped Vatican Pavilion and commemorates Pope Paul VI's visit in October 1965.

The marshy soil of Flushing Meadows sometimes reveals unique legacies of the fair. Foundations for the towers that supported the rails of the AMF Monorail occasionally pop up along the roadways in the lake area of the park today. Meadow and Willow Lakes, constructed for the 1939–1940 New York World's Fair, are two of the largest lakes on Long Island.

The moon-domed Transportation & Travel Pavilion was among many pavilions that the cash-strapped World's Fair Corporation had to pay to have demolished following the fair because its sponsors were bankrupt and could not afford to level the structure themselves. The T-shaped Port Authority Heliport had a brighter future and is used today as a popular Queens catering and banquet facility.

The Better Living Building was another pavilion that faced financial trouble during the fair. Many multiexhibitor pavilions, such as Better Living, American Interiors, and Transportation & Travel, could not compete with spectacular shows offered by the likes of IBM or Du Pont. Poor attendance often drove them to bankruptcy. The fair had to bail them out or face a public relations nightmare of explaining closed pavilions to a hostile press.

The spectacular view from the rooftop of the Better Living Building took in the fair's entire dress circle of industrial pavilions overlooking the Fountain of the Planets and the Pool of Industry. The magnificent fountain effect was removed following the fair. Today the Pool of Industry is but a stagnant moat, hardly the glorious display of decades past or the legacy of the fair envisioned by its creators.

A refreshing sight on a hot day, the cooling water sprays of the Fountains of the Fairs fronted the spectacular Bell System beyond. Following decades of disuse, the fountain effect has been restored, and it graces Flushing Meadows–Corona Park today.

The New York State Pavilion towers rise in the distance like tulips in a flower bed. The 360-degree theater is the only part of the complex restored to date. The Tent of Tomorrow, towers, and terrazzo map are a broken shambles. After several years as a roller-skating rink, the pavilion was eventually abandoned, and its multicolored roof removed when pieces of it became dangerously loose. It waits today for a savior.

The Feltman Carousel, which delighted riders young and old alike at the fair, found a home in post-fair Flushing Meadows–Corona Park. Although it no longer wears its candy-striped canopy of red and white, it still offers riders a glimpse of the kind of workmanship and craft that went into the art of building carousels.

The United States Pavilion's post-fair story is one of wasteful neglect. The $17 million structure was constructed by the federal government with the intent that it would be reused. Although suggestions for a university complex and art museum were discussed, it remained vacant for decades. Vandals nearly destroyed the pavilion over the years, from the inside out. It suffered a major fire and was finally demolished in 1977.

Today's Flushing Meadows–Corona Park is not without beauty from the legacies of the fair. Both Unisphere and *Freedom of the Human Spirit* have been restored in the past decade, with Unisphere being granted landmark status by the city. The legacies of the fair still inspire awe. Those who are too young to remember the fair may not know the history, but they understand that these remnants must represent something grand.

The floor of the Tent of Tomorrow at the New York State pavilion was an immense reproduction of a Texaco road map. This unusual backdrop was the setting for numerous concerts by bands from across the state.

Perhaps the one experience every visitor to the fair remembers is their first encounter with a Belgian waffle. The delightful pastry was the undisputed hit among fairgoers. The Belgian waffle quickly gained in popularity and today can be found on many restaurant breakfast menus.

It is surprising that such a simple recipe could make such a splash: a waffle covered with whipped cream and topped with strawberries and a little powdered sugar. The secret, fairgoers reported, was in the pastry. Whatever the reason, reminiscences about the fair often include talk of this tasty treat. Memories are made of this.

Memories of the fair also bring back thoughts of Greyhound's Glide-a-Ride trams that carried visitors around the grounds. The motorized trains were a quick and convenient form of transportation for footsore visitors. Their sleek cabs were the latest in space-age design.

Although the fair fell short of attendance expectations, a busy day could bring throngs of people to the grounds. Fairgoers strolled along the Avenue of Transportation past the Sinclair's Dinoland, United States Rubber's Ferris wheel, and the SKF Industries Pavilion. Theodore Rozek's *Forms in Space* sculpture was one of several on the fairgrounds with space-related themes.

One of the racier shows at the fair was Les Poupees de Paris, a puppet show produced by Sid and Marty Kroftt. Fair president Robert Moses was reportedly not happy with the skimpy costumes used in the show—even though the cast members were all puppets.

It was always Oktoberfest at the Lowenbrau Gardens, where visitors could be found resting their feet as they enjoyed a cold beer and German foods.

Located in the Lake Amusement Area, the Hawaiian Pavilion offered the sights, sounds, and tastes of the newest state. Demonstrations of lei making and hula dancers were among the highlights of the exhibits.

The Scott Paper Company's pavilion was aimed at users of Scott tissues, towels, and diapers. A walk through the pavilion's Enchanted Forest showed how Scott, in its own words, cared both about trees and housewives. Scott was the major paper products supplier for the fair, providing cups, napkins, and other items to the majority of restaurants and pavilions.

The traditional igloo design of the Alaska Pavilion was a contrast with the design of its neighbor, Westinghouse. There, a gleaming metal time capsule was suspended in the air, waiting to be buried for the next 5,000 years.

As impressive as any exhibit were the fair's many beautiful fountains. While the fair spent as little money as possible on building construction, it lavished money on landscaping, pools, and fountains. Memories of these beautiful displays are still vivid today, decades after the fair has ended, a testament to their design presentation.

It was not only water sprays that made the fair's fountain effects so beautiful but also the spectacular night lighting effects that made them truly memorable. The Fountains of the Fairs were found on the Main Mall that ran the length of the grounds from Unisphere to the Pool of Industry and the Bell System Pavilion. Underwater lights in the splash shields illuminated the water streams.

The Fountains of the Fairs encompassed both an east and west pond. It had a row of arching water jets on each side, directed inward toward the center of the pool. A total of 52 jet streams discharged approximately 7,200 gallons of water per minute. The fountains were neglected and vandalized in the decades following the fair. They were restored and made functional again in the late 1990s.

The central dome of the Solar Fountain, 30 feet in diameter, had colored-light ports illuminated from the interior. The dome supported a column of water 30 feet high, with 30 nozzles on a 4-foot-diameter circle. Above the central column, a star-burst 6 feet in diameter circled the dome, while wobbling jets of water simulated the sun's flaming gases.

The Lunar Fountain had arching jet streams that reached heights of 20 feet, radiating from 16 nozzles on top of an elliptical dome 24 feet in diameter at its base. A sheet of flowing water covered the dome, and lights flickered within. Its tranquil water flows were meant to suggest the appearance of the moon.

The most spectacular of all of the fair's fountains was the Fountain of the Planets and the Pool of Industry. The pool covered six and one-half acres and held 15 million gallons of water. The fountains contained some 2,000 nozzles ranging from one-half inch to over two inches in diameter. During performance peak, nearly 100 tons of water were pushed into the air at one time, with some streams soaring to 150 feet.

The circular walkway surrounding the Pool of Industry was, arguably, the fair's most heavily traveled roadway. The Pool of Industry was truly the fair's dress circle of prestige pavilions. Here, industry giants such as IBM, Bell Telephone, and General Electric presented their free, spectacular shows. Anyone who attended the fair will likely recall having seen at least one of the attractions at the Pool of Industry pavilions.

In the late afternoon, the fairgrounds reflect the light of the setting sun. It is likely that the 1964–1965 New York World's Fair will be the last of the great world's fairs to be held in the United States. Most later attempts were stymied by a lack of funding and never opened, and the smaller fairs that followed inevitably lost money.

It is nightfall, the time the fair's spectacular lighting effects are turned on. *The Rocket Thrower* is silhouetted against Unisphere in a dramatic setting of shimmering fountains and pools. It has been said that things happen too quickly today for world's fairs to be meaningful anymore. Perhaps, but people will always come to a show that is worthwhile.

Was the 1964–1965 New York World's Fair worthwhile? Ask any of the 51 million visitors who saw it and most will answer with a resounding "Yes!" Despite its flawed predictions of the future, the fair nevertheless inspired with its exhibits and beauty.

Fireworks explode and fountains soar in the nighttime finale of the 1964–1965 New York World's Fair. It was something for everybody. It was tomorrow on display in a place called Flushing Meadows in the borough of Queens. What a future the fair said this would be!